KEY STAGE 1

Year 1 | Term 3

Teaching and Learning

Science

Activity Book

Andrew Hodges

Alan Jarvis

Heather Monaghan

First published 2001

Letts Educational Ltd, The Chiswick Centre,
414 Chiswick High Road, London W4 5TF
Tel: 020 8996 3333
Fax: 020 8742 8390
www.letts-education.com

Text © Andrew Hodges, Alan Jarvis, Heather Monaghan

Series editor: Alan Jarvis
Designed, edited and produced by Gecko Limited, Cambridge
Cover design: Santamaria
Illustrations: Priscilla Lamont

British Library Cataloguing-in-Publication Data
A CIP record for this book is available from the British Library

ISBN 1 84085 545 2

Printed in the UK

Letts Educational Ltd, a division of Granada Learning Ltd. Part of the Granada Media Group.

Contents

How to use this book

In this book you will learn how to use your senses to find out about materials. You will be able to use what you have found out to sort and group the materials. Then you will learn how to test the materials to find out more about them, just like real scientists do.

Look out for these.

Some materials stick to a magnet.

The introduction tells you the most important thing to learn.

Wood makes lots of different things.

The text gives you lots of information.

This won't break. It's very strong.

Speech bubbles tell you what the children are finding out.

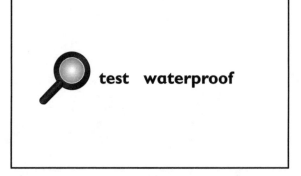

test   waterproof

You need to know what the science words mean. Look these up on page 24.

You will learn:

- the names of some materials.

- words to help you describe different materials.

- that the same material can make many different things.

- about plastic and metal.

- about wood and paper.

- about magnetic materials.

- about waterproof materials.

- how to sort and group materials.

- how to test materials.

- that you need to choose the best material to make something.

There are lots of different materials.

We make things out of materials.

Lettsdale Primary School JUMBLE SALE

This book is made of paper.

This ruler is made of wood.

Draw lots of things made of the same material. Say what the material is. Talk about what it is like.

Some things are made of more than one material.

Look at how the children are sorting different materials.
Find some things in your classroom. What are they made
from? Sort them into groups.

 **material**

What is it like?

You can use your senses to find out about materials.

Use your senses to talk about some more materials. What are they like? Are they hard and rough, or soft and squashy? What else can you say about them?

Tim cannot see the spoon. How can he guess what it is made of?

What does it feel like?

It feels cold and hard. I think it's metal.

Try this game yourself. Use some different materials. Think of some good questions to ask.

 senses   transparent

The same material can make different things.

Wood makes lots of different things.

Collect some wooden things. How are they similar? How are they different?

Lots of things are made from metal.
There are many different metals.

Collect some metal things. Try to find out what metals they are made from.

 similar

Some materials stick to a magnet.

Which things will stick to Mr Wizzo's magnetic wand?
What kind of materials are they?

Find some things that stick to a magnet. Draw them.
Then draw some things that don't stick to the magnet.

 magnet   magnetic

Lots of things are made from paper.

There are many different papers. Mrs Bell's class are sorting some into groups.

Talk about how the children are sorting their papers. How many different papers can you think of?

Find some different papers. Sort them into groups.
Make a display of the papers and label each group.

sort

You can test paper to see how strong it is.

Mrs Bell's class are testing different papers. They want to find the best paper to wrap a parcel in.

Talk about the tests the children are doing.
Tell a friend how to do one of the tests.

Can you think of another test to do?
Test some papers to see which are best.

 test

Our clothes are made from different fabrics.

Cotton keeps us cool on a hot day.

Why are these clothes good for a hot day?
What do you wear on a hot day? Why?

Wool keeps us warm on a cold day.

Why are these clothes good for a cold day?
Talk about what you might wear on a wet day.

Some materials are waterproof.

Umbrellas are made from waterproof fabric.

Can you find some waterproof fabrics?
What will you do to test them?

This umbrella is made from the wrong material.

Test some different materials to see if they are waterproof.
Tell your class what you find out.

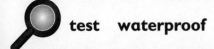

test   waterproof

You need to choose the best material to make something.

Jamila and Tom made this house.

Look at each part of the house. Talk about the materials. Did Jamila and Tom choose the best materials?

They chose different materials to make different parts of the house.

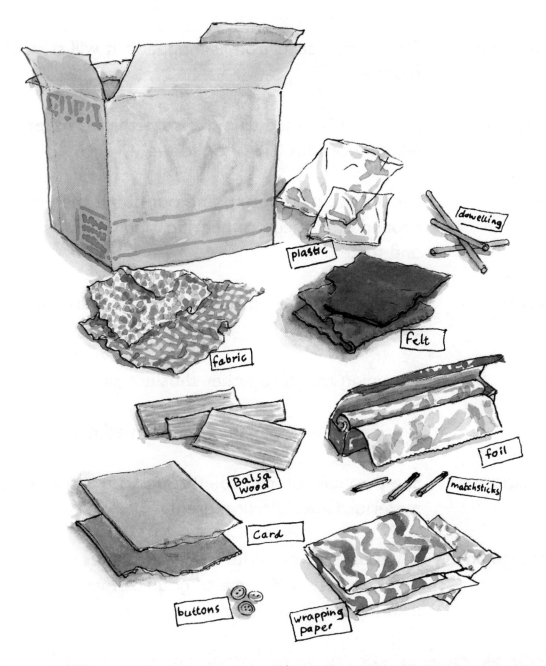

Make your own house with a friend.
Tell your class why you chose each material.

 **material**

Useful science words

magnet   A special kind of metal that some other metal things stick to.

magnetic   The metal called 'iron' is magnetic. It will stick to a magnet.

material   A material is used to make something. **Material** is also a word for 'cloth' or 'fabric'.

senses   Five senses help you to find out about the world around you. They are hearing, sight, touch, smell and taste.

similar   When things are similar they are very like each other.

sort   Grouping things together that are similar.

test   A scientific way of finding out something.

transparent   See-through. You can see through a transparent material. Glass is transparent.

waterproof   A waterproof material will not let water through it. Your house and some of your clothes are made from waterproof materials.